SENSUAL AFRICA

SENSUAL AFRICA

Photography by Joe Wuerfel
Interview with Peter Beard

EDITION STEMMLE
Zurich   New York

I dedicate this book to my family

Contents

6   Interview with Peter Beard

8   The Himba
46   The people of Heyza, Tanzania
74   The Cape Verde Islands

118   Joe Wuerfel

Interview with Peter Beard

Joe Wuerfel: What happened to the tribes in East-Africa?

Peter Beard: What happened to them is what happened to every single African alive. Loss of authenticity; interference and pressure from the western world. Missionaries, medicine and mediocrity, loss of identity, heritage, every kind of pressure, from those who have ruined the world outside.

What is the main difference between now and the time when you first visited the African continent?

When you talk about change in Africa, it's like standing in front of the mirror every day: you don't really notice yourself getting older. But if I stood in front of that mirror as I did in 1955 and then stood in front of it again today, I would probably be paralyzed with shock. There would be no way of describing the gulf between them in genuineness, diversity and the full bouquet of nature and authenticity. Now it's just a frightening Tower of Babel where instead of just talking you've got a lot of knives and guns. It's going to go deeper and deeper. As Joseph Conrad would say, "it's the horror of the horror." I don't think it's going to get a lot better in East and Central Africa—maybe in Botswana and Namibia—that's going to be very nice down there, I think, because they've got a very homogeneous tribal situation, and the bills are paid by De Beers. According to our standards, the Africans live in misery. But they lived in this so-called "misery" for centuries before we came. The interference in the biology of life doesn't work. It's just a disaster, but it can't be prevented. And that's the problem!

There are plans by the Namibian government to build a dam on Himbaland (Kaokoland) that would destroy hundreds of their ancestors' graves, and also prime vegetation. The Himbas believe in the holy spirit of their ancestors.

I'm afraid that's what they call in East-Africa the galloping rot, always the perfect excuse for everything. And everybody's got an answer and the lavaflow goes in one direction. The truth is that any African politician has to make a terrible decision, because every African has so many relatives. You talk about the troubles with school fees or getting into office. You've got one or two brothers, and that guarantees you fifty begging relatives. They all want jobs, they all want cuts, they all want to be out of their misery and horror.

When did the so-called "galloping rot" start?

The galloping rot started with the missionaries and the hunters, the early explorers.

Trying to bring them Western beliefs?

Yes, that was the beginning of the process of interference. Joe, just read Joseph Conrad's *Heart of Darkness*, I urge you! You have to read it, and you'll get amazing quotes about Africa.

What happened to the game?

It's going to be pushed and pressured. The zoological garden is becoming the zoo. Mankind has no comprehension of art. And then you will have beyond that a permanent motorized procession.

You mean a organized spectacle of fake wild-life?

Completely manipulated, completely pressured, completely contrived—everything that is not artistic. Mankind has no comprehension of art. The only reason why art is good is that it is a barometer of civilization. If you are in the history of art, that's culture. We have no visual appreciation of art. But what people want is very regrettable, and I would say the destruction of the world is on a par with our lack of aesthetic. We don't have a visual sense. Darwin was really correct: in art everything is useless. He was showing that art hasn't a survival benefit.

So he meant it is not necessary to have art?

Right, all that is certain is that males exploring territories developed an artistic achievement; women haven't really done it yet. Women are still close enough to nature. "Vive la difference" I would say. I don't know why we are so obsessed with unisex. The whole point is not to get messed up, and when you get messed up as with over-density and stress, the first result is a separation of the sexes.

What can you do as a photographer?

First of all I regret even being in the medium of photography because it's true that I'm only interested in the subject matter. I'm not interested in photography. I'm not interested in illustrating or being a messenger-boy, or being concerned with joining Magnum. I just want to pursue a subject matter that I am interested in. Period. I am selfish, and it is just a coincidence that one of the best photographic opportunities that I have had was the big elephant die-off in Tsabo. It was illegal for me to go in there on the ground, so I had to be in an airplane. And being in an airplane got me thousands of carcasses, and they are great, because they are great subject matter, they are sculptures. The pictures of the elephants have been my best pictures. They happened to be a message, but I didn't want them to be a message.

They didn't allow you to go in there on foot?

That's right. No photography.

Why?

Because the die-off was the final stroke of my assault. I was working for the National Park in 1964. We had been marking elephants, playing this little game. They had to figure out how many elephants were eating the park. The park was disappearing. It had had a long history and slowly the park was being eaten by overpopulation of elephants. They had the first die-off of rhinos, a big die-off in 1971–1974 with up to 30.000 elephants. After losing all the bush, first you eat everything, then you die. That's important for human beings too, that's how we manage our environment—*no* management. I used to work for wildlife services and was involved in the shooting of elephants in Uganda.

Did you live together with the Masai?

Yes, I lived with them on top of the Loitas (high plateau), and I participated in the first outdoor medicineman ceremonies with giraffe-bone-pipes and fantastic elephant-tusk pipes. We did a book about all that called *Art of the Masai*, published by Alfred Knopf. It was a major thing.

We don't see how artistically the tribes live, the way they use nature. They only take away as much as they need.

We usually figure it out in a direct ratio to the degree to which it is too late. And that's the thing with conservation. We started to save the rhino in a direct ratio to the degree to which it was too late. We started to save the elephant in a direct ratio to the degree to which it was too late.

Economic interests are too powerful?

Too much pressure, too much manipulation, distance from nature, artificiality, lack of experience. We are entering the robot digital computerworld of the future, and it's going to be a real website of artificiality, plastic, fake.

Montauk, 3th January 2000

7

The Himba

Married Himba woman,
near Purros, Kaokoland, Namibia

The Himba are semi-nomadic herdsmen who live in Kaokoland in the north of Namibia. Their forefathers, Herero-speaking shepherds, wandered from the Angolan province of Mocamedes, where related groups still live, probably around the mid-16th century. About 1750, most of the Hereros gravitated towards the center of Namibia. The Himba emerged mainly from the groups which remained in the north. Today, Himba and Herero live together in harmony.

Although the two groups are related to each other, they differ starkly in appearance. Small external features used to distinguish them up to the arrival of the German colonizers. Hair-style, head-dresses and clothing followed a centuries-old tradition. However, the wives of the German colonials were shocked by the nakedness of the native population, and they tried to persuade them to adopt a new style of clothing. In the course of time, more and more Herero men and women began to wear Wilhelmine dress, and the head-coverings of the colonials. The Himba maintained their traditional ways.

Himba nomad women never wash as long as they live. Instead, they use a paste made of butter-fat mixed with powdered ferruginous stone *(otjize)*. This stone is only found at the place of the same name. Continuously massaging the skin with this mixture is not only a question of beauty—it also helps to protect the skin and serves as a substitute for scarce water. The women wear beautiful decorations made of iron, copper and brass. Their clothes consist of brief loincloths made of calf-skin. Many of them wear the conical shell of a Ngoma snail on a long necklace. This creature is only found in one particular place in Angola, on the cold Atlantic coast. When a Himba man wants to get married, he sets off on foot on a pilgrimage to this place which lasts several days, to find a shell for his bride.

The hair-styles and head-dresses of the Himba always convey meaning. Young nubile women wear two plaits which stick out on the front of their heads. These symbolize the horns of the Himba's sacred cattle. To signal their readiness for marriage (a period which coincides with the onset of menstruation) they later go on to wear a small, decorated leather crown on their head. Married women, by contrast, wear a leather cap. Kaokoland belongs to the last wild unspoiled regions of Africa. Due to the dangerous Skeleton Coast in the west, a dry, rugged chain of mountains in the east and the merciless Namibian desert in the south, the region in very difficult of access and hence remained completely unexplored until well into the twentieth century. Until 1963 the Ova Tjimba, a tribe related to the Himba, lived as hunters and gatherers in the remote Baynes and Otjihipa mountains, using only stone tools and weapons. Today the traditional lifestyle of the Himba is under increasing threat from the pervasive influence of our western culture and from profit-motivated exploration. One of the last remaining areas of the old, real Africa is being dragged into the modern world. It would be nice if the unstoppable developments in the name of so-called progress could be determined by the Himba themselves, so that they would not be robbed of their dignity and self-respect.

2
Girl in her ozondjuwo (hut),
Kaokoland, Namibia

10
Himba boy,
near the Hoarusib River, Kaokoland, Namibia

11
Girl on donkey,
Hoarusib, Kaokoland, Namibia

Himba woman with shell,
Otjihende, Kaokoland, Namibia

14/15
Baobabs,
Kaokoland, Namibia

16
Girl with jewellery,
near Purros, Kaokoland, Namibia

17
Portrait of a Himba girl,
Kaokoland, Namibia

Girl laughing,
near the Kunene River, Kaokoland, Namibia

Girls walking,
near the Kunene River, Kaokoland, Namibia

Unmarried girls,
near the Kunene River, Kaokoland, Namibia

Small boy,
near Otjize, Kaokoland, Namibia

26
Young girl,
Kaokoland, Namibia

27
Young girl in her ozonganda
(estate on a rubbish dump),
Kaokoland, Namibia

28
Himba youth with ondatu (plait),
Kaokoland, Namibia

29
Leopard,
Kaokoland, Namibia

Girl in her ozondjuwo (hut),
Kaokoland, Namibia

32
Two girls,
Otjihende, Kaokoland, Namibia

33
Himba youth,
Otjize, Kaokoland, Namibia

Himba girl with ohumba (shell),
Otjihende, Kaokoland, Namibia

36
Old woman,
Okongwati, Kaokoland, Namibia

37
Girls' hands,
Otjihende, Kaokoland, Namibia

38/39
Zebras,
Etoshapfanne, Kaokoland, Namibia

40
Himba youth,
Kaokoland, Namibia

41
Nursing mother with ekori (bridal wreath),
near Epupa Falls, Kaokoland, Namibia

42
Himba chief,
near Opuwo, Kaokoland, Namibia

43
Herero woman,
Purros, Kaokoland, Namibia

44/45
Herero women,
near Opuwo, Kaokoland, Namibia

The people of Heyza, Tanzania

Heyza is an isolated village in the southern highlands of Tanzania, bordering on Malawi and Zambia to the south. Its people are the Nyha. This tribe has inhabited the region for centuries. Their clay huts are widely scattered throughout the remote mountain region.

The Nyha believe in the power of witchcraft as well as in the healing power of their medicine-men. They carry their sick to the home of the healer. Very often it is too late, because the trip through the bush is too long. When somebody dies, all the members of the family shave off their hair—including women and children—as a mark of respect for the person who has died. During the period of mourning they hold their hands up to their faces, close their eyes and thus express to the arriving funeral guests the sorrow they feel at the death of their loved one.

The Nyha have been able to survive in this harsh and beautiful land for centuries; they have managed to live through droughts and floods, on the absolute minimum. However, they are not as hopeless as may appear by our standards. In many ways, they are heading in the right direction—such as in education, agricultural programs, water supply and basic standards of medicine. They are evolving African solutions.

Give me black souls,
Let them be black
Or chocolate brown
Or make the color of dust
Dustlike
Browner than sand
But if you can
Please keep them black
Black.

Give me some drums
Let them be three
Or maybe four
And make them black
Dirty and black
Of wood
But if you will
Just make them peal
Peal.

Frank Kobina Parkes
from: African Heaven, Songs of the Wilderness

Landscape,
Tanzania

48

Masai,
Tanzania

52
Nyha woman,
Heyza, Tanzania

53
Woman's foot,
Heyza, Tanzania

54
Man with pig,
Heyza, Tanzania

55
A chief with his wife,
Heyza, Tanzania

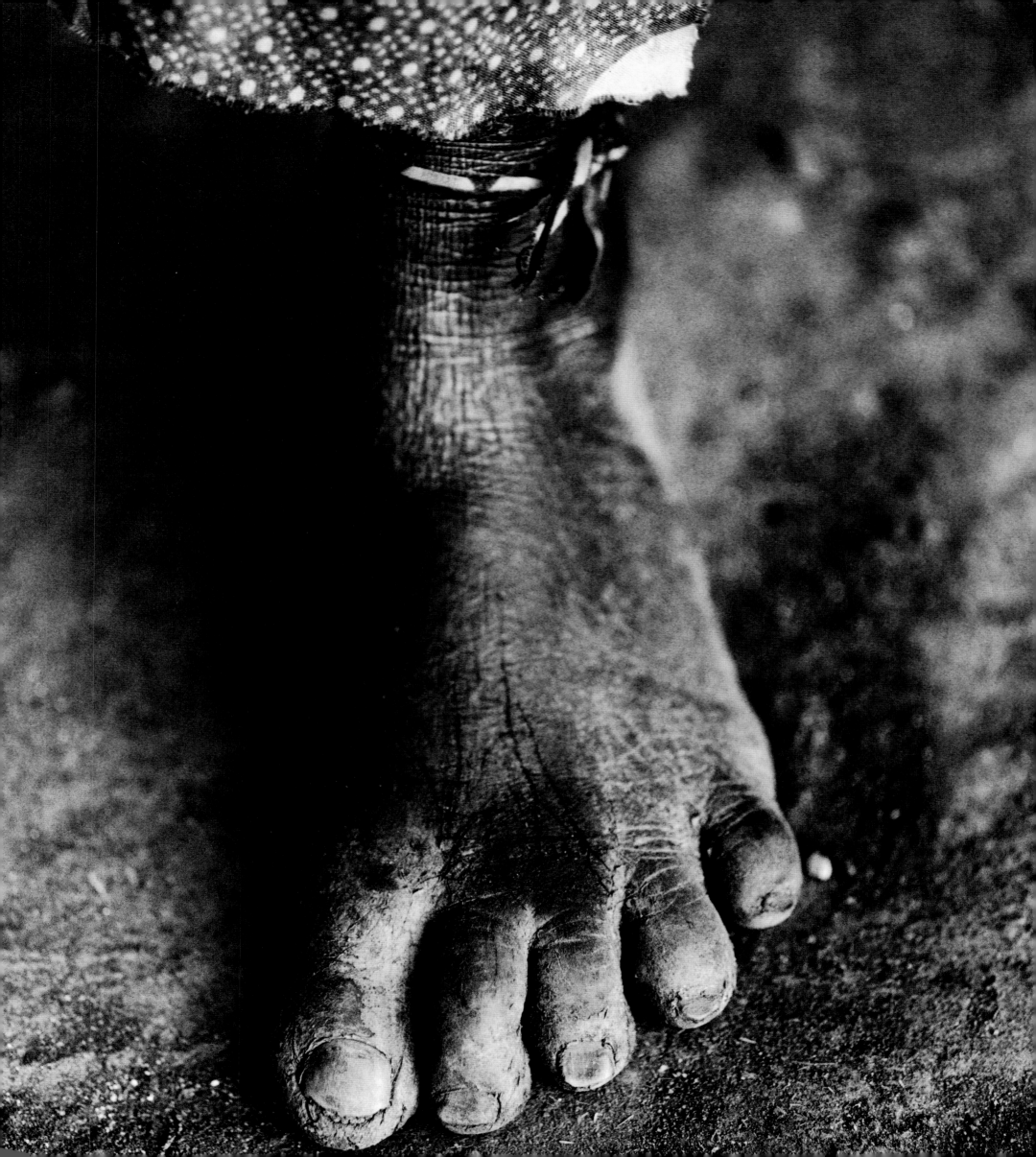

Siblings,
Heyza, Tanzania

Lions,
Mikumi, Tanzania

60
Masai,
Tanzania

61
Masai,
Tanzania

62/63
Woman balancing firewood,
Heyza, Tanzania

Medicine-man with his wife,
Heyza, Tanzania

Women complaining,
Heyza, Tanzania

Woman posing,
Heyza, Tanzania

70
Two women,
Heyza, Tanzania

71
Storage huts,
Heyza, Tanzania

On the way to Heyza,
Tanzania

The Cape Verde Islands

The islands are situated in the Atlantic, 400 miles from the western coast of Senegal. It's first people have been brought as slaves from the African continent from where they started their tragic journey into the new world. Different periods (Portuguese colonization, pirates and sailors from all over the world) have created a melting pot of races. There are 15 islands, six of them still unpopulated. They vary from Sahel-landscapes to tropical vegetations. People of the islands have a unique mentality. Their love for music is a basic content of their everyday life. It is based on the songs of the slaves with influences of Portuguese Fado and Brazilian traditional rhythms. The Republic of the Cape Verde Islands has no political prisoners. The Cape Verde Islands constitute one of the few countries in Africa with a functioning democracy. They are also one of the poorest countries in the world.

The philosophy of Nununa the fisherman

Every morning when I say my prayers I thank God that our islands are so poor—we have no mineral resources at all. No one is interested in declaring war onus, and we are happy; the only thing we are short of is a little rain.
But there are diamonds on the Cape Verde Islands—lots of them—our women!

Petit pays (Little Country)
Text: Wando da Cruz
Melody: Césaria Évora

In the sky you are a star
That does not shine.
On the sea you are the sand
That does not moisten.
Scattered throughout the world,
Rocks and sea,
Avid land, full of love,
And Morna and Caldera,
Sweet land, full of love,
And Batuque and Funana.
Such nostalgia,
Such endless nostalgia.
My little country,
I love you so.

Fishermen,
San Pedro, São Vicente

Girl,
Praia, Santiago

82
Woman's feet in water,
Espargos, Sal

83
Young woman,
Espargos, Sal

Four women,
Mindelo, São Vicente

Woman washing,
Espargos, Sal

88
In prison,
Tarafal, Praia, Santiago

89
Lobster processing,
Palmeira, Sal

Girl in harbour,
Mindelo, São Vicente

92
Girl with fish,
Palmeira, Sal

93
Girl with firewood,
Palmeira, Sal

94
Moslem woman,
Praia, Santiago

95
Market woman,
Assomado, Praia, Santiago

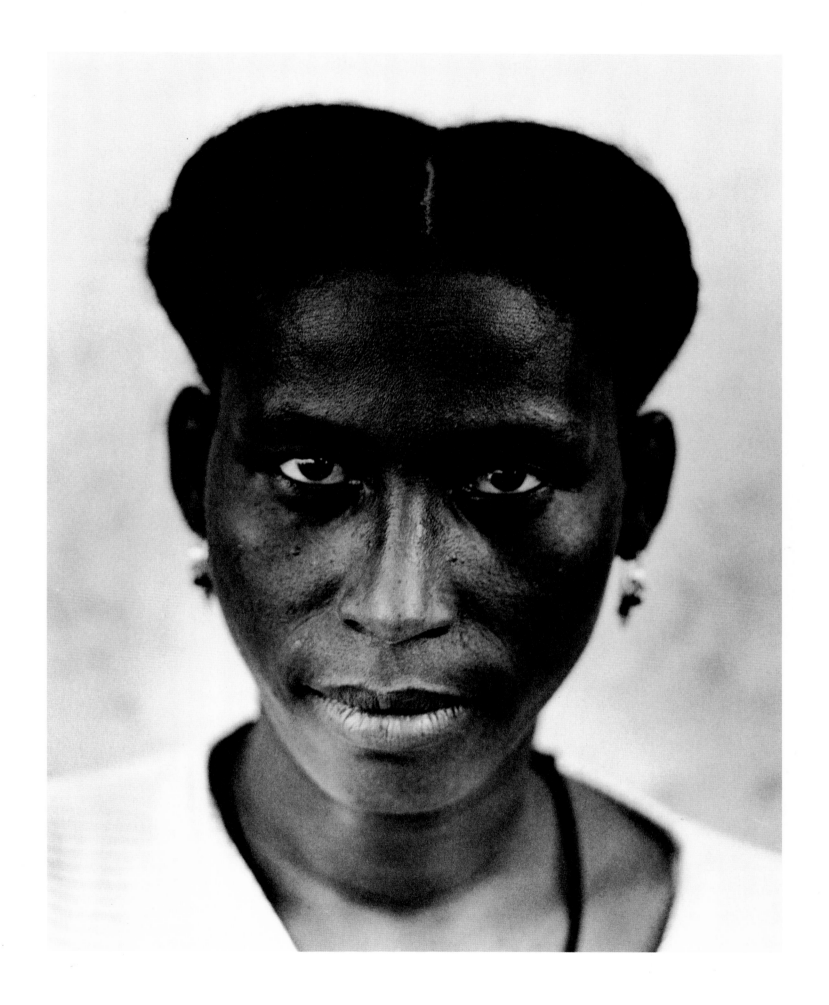

Nununa, fisherman with wooden cross,
Mindelo, São Vicente

98/99
Fish-market,
Mindelo, São Vicente

Young woman,
Praia, Santiago

102
Girl with turban,
Praia, Santiago

103
Girl with fish in her mouth,
Praia, Santiago

104/105
Child,
São Filipe, Fogo

Mother and child,
Mindelo, São Vicente

Fisherman's son,
Salamansa, São Vicente

Musician,
Monte Verde, São Vicente

112
Mama Fogo,
Chã das Caldeiras, Fogo

113
Small boy in the fish-market,
Mindelo, São Vicente

114
Two angels,
San Pedro, São Vicente

115
Women,
Belem, Mindelo, São Vicente

116
Boxer,
Mindelo, São Vicente

117
Wreck,
Porto Grande, Mindelo, São Vicente

My personal interest in Africa began with the joy of taking photographs of its outstanding people and landscapes. Until I was asked to photograph the village and its people for a charity and self-help organization in Tanzania, I was only interested in the subject matter. I found that Africa is not the continent of an idyllic life lived close to nature which we middle-class westerners like to believe. Talking to Peter Beard made me understand the history of the east African tribes, and the tragedy that has happened to African wildlife. It made me understand that our western culture tries to make almost everything conform to our standards. I woke up, I took photographs of endangered tribes who are trying to defend their freedom. They are making a stand against alcohol-related diseases and government interests such as tourism. For most of them it's too late, as well as for the wild life in almost every region. The game-parks are fenced, and do not allow the animals to move around freely. Their very existence is guaranteed by our own presence. Unfortunately, we can not stop this development, that began with the first explorers.

My journey started in Tanzania. I crossed the state to its south-western border, where I lived with the people of Heyza. I was heading for Namibia, to the Kaokofeld on the border with Angola. I lived with the Himba, one of the last semi-nomadic tribes in Africa. Then I landed on the Cape Verde Islands, 400 miles from the western coast of Senegal. Africa is a continent with many facets—both difficult to get to grips with and fascinating at the same time. It seems to me that this is only the beginning of the journey.

Joe Wuerfel

1952	Born in Stuttgart, Germany.
1970–74	After completing school, assistant to Franz Lazi, Stuttgart, Germany.
1975	Assistant to Rudolf Schmutz, Zurich, Switzerland.
1979	Meets Jean Loup Sieff; works with Brett Weston, Carmel, California. Takes up work as a free-lance photographer.
1980	First extended trips across the United States. Trip to Italy.
1986	Work for the Polaroid Collection, Boston, Massachusetts.
1987	Architectural photographs for Ettore Sottsass, Milan, Italy.
1988–95	Commissions for various international campaigns.
1990	Moves to Miami Beach, Florida, where he now lives.
1996	Extended trips to Africa for an international campaign. Lives in the bush in the Okawango Delta, Botswana.
1997–98	Trip to Tanzania for the Wakina Mama na Watoto Foundation, Heyza, and the Swiss Tropical Institute, Basel, Switzerland.
1999	Two month trip to Cape Verde Islands. Trip to Namibia and Angola. Lives with the Himba in Kaokoland.

Selected Solo Exhibitions

1982	*Natura Morte*, Nikon Gallery, Zurich, Switzerland
1984	*American Landscapes*, Nikon Gallery, Zurich, Switzerland *American Landscapes*, Canon Gallery, Amsterdam, The Netherlands
1997/98	*The People of Heyza*, Swiss Tropical Institute, Basel, Switzerland
1999	*The People of Heyza*, The National Museum, Dar es Salaam, Tanzania

Publications

1985	*Photoedition 7, Joe Wuerfel*, Verlag Photographie, Schaffhausen, Switzerland
1997/98	*The People of Heyza*, Calendar project for the Swiss Tropical Institute, Basel, Switzerland
1999	*Karibu Africa*, Calendar project for the Wakina Mama na Watoto Foundation, Heyza, and the Swiss Tropical Institute, Basel, Switzerland

I wish to express my heartfelt thanks to Peter Beard for his assistance.

I owe a special debt of thanks to my Himba friend Materepo, who taught me so much about his people, and to my friend Bernd, without whose help my trips and the realization of this project would not have been possible.

My thanks also go to the Himba people of Kaokoland, the people of Heyza, and the Wakina Mama na Watoto Foundation, Tanzania, who entertained me with generosity and spontaneity.

I would also like to thank Peter Tanney, Lowell Tindell, Gert Eltering, Randy Mitchell (dark room) and Daniel (Premier Vu) for their co-operation.

Copyright © 2000 by Stemmle Publishers GmbH/
EDITION STEMMLE, Thalwil/Zurich (Switzerland) and
New York

Reproductions copyright by Joe Wuerfel, Miami Beach
Texts copyright by Peter Beard, New York, Joe Wuerfel, Miami Beach, and Bernd Stickroth, Zurich, Switzerland

Translation from the German by John B. Walmsley
Editorial direction by Sara Schindler
Layout and Typography by Giorgio Chiappa
Lithography by pp.digitech ag, Adliswil/Zurich, Switzerland and Alpha Druckereiservice GmbH, Radolfzell, Germany
Printed by Spefa Druck AG, Zurich, Switzerland
Bound by Buchbinderei Burkhardt AG, Mönchaltorf/Zurich, Switzerland

ISBN 3-908163-13-7